Altcoin Investments: a guide to Crypto Success

INDEX

Chapter 1 – Introduction..3

Chapter 2 - Understanding Altcoins 5

Chapter 2.1 - Examining Prominent Altcoins..........10

Chapter 3 - Market Analysis for Investment...........20

Chapter 3.1 - Risk Management Strategies.............25

Chapter 3.2 - Portfolio Diversification....................30

Chapter 4 - Navigating Regulatory Challenges........35

Chapter 5 - Future Outlook and Emerging Technologies..41

Chapter 6 – A Case Study..46

Chapter 7 – Conclusions..52

The purpose of this ebook is to offer a practical guide for individuals keen on delving into altcoin investment opportunities. It aims to simplify the intricacies surrounding altcoin investments and furnish readers with a structured method for researching and assessing potential investment prospects. Through grasping the fundamental principles and strategies delineated in this ebook, readers will be more adept at navigating the altcoin market and making informed investment choices.

Andrew J. Burns

Chapter 1 – Introduction

"Altcoin Investments: a guide to Crypto Success" is a comprehensive ebook designed to guide both new and experienced cryptocurrency investors through the world of alternative cryptocurrencies, or altcoins.
The book explores the rising popularity of altcoins and their potential beyond Bitcoin.

Through meticulous examination, it delves into various prominent altcoins like Ethereum, Ripple, Litecoin, and Cardano, detailing their unique features, underlying technology, and investment potential.

The ebook not only educates readers on altcoins but also provides insights into successful cryptocurrency investing, offering guidance on identifying promising altcoins, evaluating growth potential, and managing risk in volatile market conditions. It also covers strategies for portfolio diversification and maximizing investment returns.

Authored by experts, the book combines research, real-life examples, and actionable advice to empower readers to make informed decisions in the altcoin market, catering to both seasoned traders and newcomers alike.

The ebook "**Altcoin Investments: a guide to Crypto Success**" covers several key topics essential for navigating the world of alternative cryptocurrencies.

Donald Ross

Chapter 2 - Understanding Altcoins

Understanding Altcoins: It provides an in-depth explanation of altcoins and their significance within the cryptocurrency ecosystem, offering clarity on their role beyond Bitcoin.

Understanding Altcoins: Exploring the World of Cryptocurrency Diversity

In the ever-expanding universe of cryptocurrencies, Bitcoin is often the star player, capturing headlines and attention with its meteoric rise and occasional dips. However, beyond the shadow of Bitcoin lies a diverse ecosystem of digital currencies collectively known as altcoins. Understanding altcoins is essential for anyone delving deeper into the realm of cryptocurrency, as they offer unique features, use cases, and opportunities for investment and innovation.

Altcoins, a portmanteau of "alternative" and "coins," encompass any cryptocurrency other than Bitcoin. They emerged in the wake of Bitcoin's success, aiming to address perceived shortcomings or explore different technological approaches. While some altcoins are mere clones or variations of Bitcoin, others introduce novel features such as enhanced privacy, smart contract functionality, or improved scalability.

One of the most well-known altcoins is Ethereum. Launched in 2015 by Vitalik Buterin, Ethereum introduced smart contracts, enabling developers to build decentralized applications (dApps) and execute self-executing contracts without the need for intermediaries. This innovation opened the floodgates to a multitude of projects across various industries, from decentralized finance (DeFi) to non-fungible tokens (NFTs).

Litecoin, often referred to as the silver to Bitcoin's gold, was one of the earliest altcoins, created in 2011 by Charlie Lee. It shares many similarities with Bitcoin but offers faster transaction times and a different hashing algorithm, catering to users who prioritize speed and efficiency in transactions.

Privacy-focused altcoins like Monero and Zcash prioritize anonymity and fungibility, aiming to provide users with financial privacy by obscuring transaction details and shielding the identities of senders and recipients. These coins appeal to individuals seeking greater confidentiality in their financial transactions, particularly in an era of increased surveillance and data tracking.

Beyond these prominent examples, the world of altcoins is vast and diverse. Some coins focus on specific industries or use cases, such as decentralized storage (Filecoin), supply chain management (VeChain), or gaming (Enjin Coin). Others experiment with consensus mechanisms, governance models, or environmental sustainability, pushing the boundaries of what's possible within the cryptocurrency space.

Investing in altcoins carries both opportunities and risks. While some altcoins have generated substantial returns for early investors, others have faded into obscurity or succumbed to scams and market manipulation. Conducting thorough research, assessing the team behind the project, evaluating the technology and community support, and exercising caution are essential when considering altcoin investments.

Furthermore, the volatility of the altcoin market can be significant, with prices subject to rapid fluctuations driven by factors such as market sentiment, regulatory developments, technological advancements, and macroeconomic trends. As such, investors should be prepared for wild price swings and exercise discipline in managing their portfolios.

Understanding altcoins requires an appreciation of their diversity, innovation, and potential impact on the future of finance and technology. While Bitcoin remains the flagship cryptocurrency, altcoins continue to push the boundaries of what's possible in the digital asset space, offering alternative solutions and avenues for exploration in the quest for decentralized innovation.

Chapter 2.1 - Examining Prominent Altcoins

Examining Prominent Altcoins: The book thoroughly examines leading altcoins such as Ethereum, Ripple, Litecoin, and Cardano, detailing their features, functionalities, and real-world applications.

Examining Prominent Altcoins

In the dynamic world of cryptocurrencies, Bitcoin may have been the first star, but it's far from the only celestial body. Enter altcoins, the alternative digital currencies that have proliferated since Bitcoin's inception. While Bitcoin remains the most well-known and widely adopted cryptocurrency, a plethora of altcoins have emerged, each with its unique features, purposes, and potentials. Let's delve into the examination of some of the most prominent altcoins that have captivated the attention of investors and enthusiasts alike.

1. Ethereum (ETH):

Often hailed as the silver to Bitcoin's gold, Ethereum stands out as one of the most significant altcoins. Launched in 2015 by Vitalik Buterin, Ethereum introduced the concept of smart contracts, enabling developers to build decentralized applications (DApps) on its blockchain. This capability has propelled Ethereum into the forefront of the decentralized finance (DeFi) movement, facilitating a wide array of financial services such as lending, borrowing, and decentralized exchanges.

2. Binance Coin (BNB):

Born out of the Binance cryptocurrency exchange, Binance Coin has rapidly ascended the ranks to become one of the top altcoins by market capitalization. Initially created as a utility token for discounted trading fees on the Binance platform, BNB has evolved into a multifaceted asset. With the launch of Binance Smart Chain, BNB has expanded its utility to include participation in decentralized finance (DeFi) protocols, NFT marketplaces, and more.

3. Cardano (ADA):

Founded by Charles Hoskinson, one of Ethereum's co-founders, Cardano aims to address the scalability, interoperability, and sustainability issues plaguing many blockchain networks. Utilizing a research-driven approach, Cardano seeks to offer a secure and scalable platform for the development of DApps and smart contracts. With its emphasis on peer-reviewed research and formal verification, Cardano has garnered attention for its commitment to academic rigor and technological innovation.

4. Solana (SOL):

Solana has emerged as a prominent player in the realm of high-performance blockchain networks. Leveraging a unique combination of technologies, including a proof-of-history (PoH) consensus mechanism and a Byzantine fault tolerance (BFT) consensus algorithm, Solana boasts impressive scalability and low transaction costs. This makes it an attractive platform for applications requiring high throughput and fast transaction finality, such as decentralized exchanges and gaming platforms.

5. Polkadot (DOT):

Conceived by Ethereum co-founder Dr. Gavin Wood, Polkadot aims to facilitate interoperability and scalability across multiple blockchains. Operating as a heterogeneous multi-chain framework, Polkadot enables different blockchains to communicate and share data securely. This interoperability opens up a plethora of possibilities for cross-chain asset transfers, decentralized finance (DeFi) applications, and decentralized autonomous organizations (DAOs).

Examining these prominent altcoins provides a glimpse into the diverse array of projects and innovations shaping the cryptocurrency landscape. While Bitcoin remains the undisputed king of digital gold, altcoins continue to push the boundaries of what's possible with blockchain technology, driving forward the evolution of decentralized finance, decentralized applications, and the broader crypto ecosystem.

Ethereum, Ripple, Litecoin: Exploring Three Prominent Altcoins

In the dynamic world of cryptocurrencies, Ethereum, Ripple, and Litecoin stand out as three prominent altcoins, each with its unique characteristics, use cases, and contributions to the crypto ecosystem. Let's delve into the intricacies of these digital assets and explore what sets them apart.

1. Ethereum (ETH):

Often regarded as the pioneer of smart contracts and decentralized applications (DApps), Ethereum has solidified its position as one of the most influential altcoins since its launch in 2015. Founded by Vitalik Buterin, Ethereum introduced a groundbreaking concept that extended beyond the limitations of Bitcoin's blockchain. By enabling developers to create programmable contracts and applications, Ethereum sparked a wave of innovation in the decentralized finance (DeFi), non-fungible tokens (NFTs), and decentralized autonomous organizations (DAOs) sectors.

At the core of Ethereum's functionality is its native cryptocurrency, Ether (ETH), which serves as both a medium of exchange and a fuel for executing smart contracts on the Ethereum network. Ethereum's ongoing transition from a proof-of-work (PoW) to a proof-of-stake (PoS) consensus mechanism, through the Ethereum 2.0 upgrade, aims to improve scalability, energy efficiency, and security, positioning Ethereum for long-term sustainability and growth.

2. Ripple (XRP):

Ripple, founded in 2012, offers a unique approach to blockchain technology, focusing primarily on facilitating cross-border payments and remittances. Unlike many other cryptocurrencies, Ripple's protocol, known as the RippleNet, does not rely on mining or proof-of-work mechanisms. Instead, it utilizes a consensus protocol called the Ripple Protocol Consensus Algorithm (RPCA), which enables fast and cost-effective transactions.

XRP, the native cryptocurrency of the Ripple network, plays a crucial role in facilitating transactions and liquidity within the Ripple ecosystem. Ripple's partnerships with financial institutions and payment service providers have positioned XRP as a viable solution for international money transfers, offering lower fees and faster settlement times compared to traditional banking systems.

3. Litecoin (LTC):

Created by Charlie Lee in 2011, Litecoin emerged as one of the earliest Bitcoin alternatives, often referred to as "digital silver" to Bitcoin's "digital gold." Litecoin shares many similarities with Bitcoin, including its proof-of-work consensus mechanism and supply cap of 84 million coins. However, Litecoin distinguishes itself through its faster block generation time and a different hashing algorithm (Scrypt), which enhances transaction speed and accessibility.

While Litecoin initially aimed to complement Bitcoin by offering faster and cheaper transactions, it has evolved to encompass a broader range of use cases, including peer-to-peer payments, microtransactions, and store-of-value. Litecoin's adoption of technologies like the Lightning Network further enhances its scalability and utility, paving the way for seamless and efficient cryptocurrency transactions.

In conclusion, Ethereum, Ripple, and Litecoin exemplify the diversity and innovation present in the world of altcoins. Whether it's Ethereum's smart contract capabilities, Ripple's focus on cross-border payments, or Litecoin's fast and accessible transactions, each altcoin contributes to the ongoing evolution of blockchain technology and reshapes the landscape of digital finance. As the crypto ecosystem continues to evolve, these altcoins are poised to play pivotal roles in shaping the future of decentralized finance and beyond.

Chapter 3 - Market Analysis for Investment

Market Analysis for Investment: Readers learn to analyze market trends and indicators to identify potential investment opportunities within the altcoin space, enabling them to make informed investment decisions.

In the ever-evolving landscape of cryptocurrency, altcoins continue to captivate investors with their potential for exponential growth and innovation. However, navigating the altcoin market requires more than just luck. It demands a deep understanding of market analysis techniques to discern promising investment opportunities from fleeting trends.

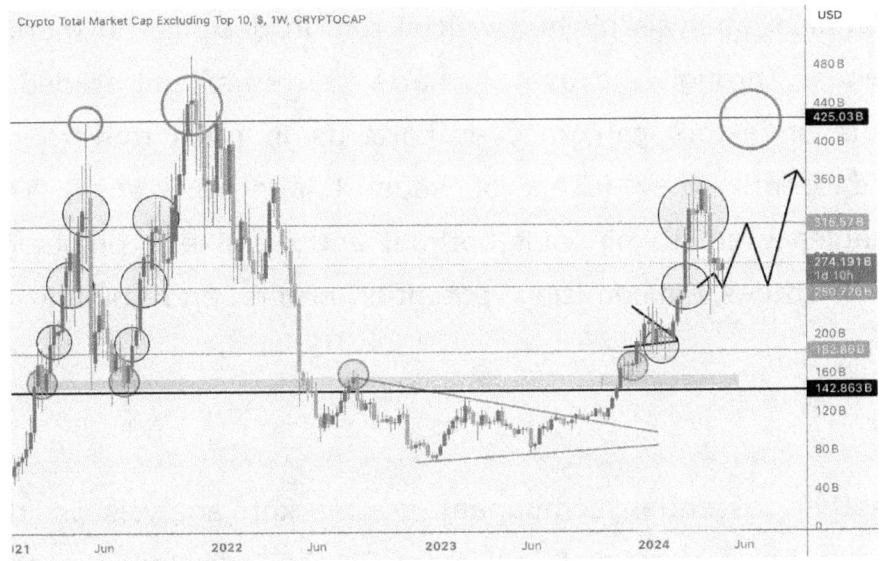

Market analysis serves as the compass for investors, guiding them through the turbulent seas of volatility and uncertainty. By examining market trends and indicators, investors can gain invaluable insights into the potential trajectories of altcoins, empowering them to make well-informed investment decisions.

One of the fundamental aspects of market analysis is trend analysis. Trends in the altcoin market can reveal valuable information about the sentiments of investors and the direction in which prices are likely to move. By identifying trends, investors can capitalize on upward momentum or protect themselves from potential downturns.

Technical analysis plays a crucial role in deciphering market trends. Through the use of charts, patterns, and statistical tools, investors can uncover patterns in price movements and identify key levels of support and resistance. This enables them to pinpoint optimal entry and exit points for their trades, maximizing potential profits and minimizing losses.

Another essential component of market analysis is the examination of market indicators. These indicators, ranging from simple moving averages to complex oscillators, provide valuable signals about the strength and direction of market trends. By analyzing these indicators in conjunction with price action, investors can gain deeper insights into market dynamics and anticipate potential trend reversals or continuations.

Furthermore, sentiment analysis offers a unique perspective on market dynamics by gauging the collective mood of investors. Social media platforms, forums, and news articles can serve as valuable sources of sentiment data, helping investors assess market sentiment and identify potential market-moving events or trends.

In addition to technical analysis and sentiment analysis, fundamental analysis plays a vital role in evaluating the long-term viability and potential of altcoin investments. By examining factors such as project fundamentals, technology, team expertise, and market adoption, investors can assess the intrinsic value of altcoins and make informed decisions about their investment strategies.

Ultimately, mastering market analysis is a continuous learning process that requires dedication, patience, and a willingness to adapt to changing market conditions. By honing their analytical skills and staying informed about the latest developments in the altcoin space, investors can navigate the market with confidence and unlock the potential for significant returns on their investments.

Chapter 3.1 - Risk Management Strategies

Risk Management Strategies: It offers insights into implementing effective risk management strategies tailored for altcoin investments, helping readers mitigate potential losses in volatile market conditions.

Navigating Altcoin Investments: Effective Risk Management Strategies

In the world of cryptocurrency investing, the allure of altcoins is undeniable. With the potential for high returns and groundbreaking innovation, altcoins attract investors eager to capitalize on the next big opportunity. However, amidst the promise lies inherent risk, as the altcoin market is notorious for its volatility and unpredictability. To navigate this landscape successfully, investors must implement effective risk management strategies tailored specifically for altcoin investments.

Understanding the unique risks associated with altcoin investing is the first step towards effective risk management. Altcoins often exhibit extreme price fluctuations, driven by factors such as market sentiment, technological developments, regulatory changes, and macroeconomic trends. Additionally, the lack of regulatory oversight and liquidity in many altcoin markets can exacerbate volatility, amplifying both potential gains and losses.

One of the most fundamental risk management strategies for altcoin investors is portfolio diversification. Diversifying across a range of altcoins helps spread risk and minimize the impact of adverse price movements in any single asset. However, it's essential to strike a balance between diversification and concentration, ensuring that the portfolio is not overly exposed to any one asset or sector.

Setting clear investment goals and risk tolerance levels is another critical aspect of effective risk management. By defining specific objectives and establishing risk limits, investors can avoid emotional decision-making and adhere to a disciplined investment approach. This involves determining acceptable levels of loss and implementing stop-loss orders or hedging strategies to mitigate downside risk.

Furthermore, conducting thorough due diligence on altcoin projects before investing is essential for mitigating risks. This includes evaluating factors such as project fundamentals, technology, team expertise, community support, and market adoption. By thoroughly researching potential investments, investors can make more informed decisions and avoid falling victim to scams or fraudulent schemes.

Implementing disciplined trading strategies is paramount for managing risk in the volatile altcoin market. This includes maintaining a clear exit strategy for each trade, whether based on predetermined price targets, technical indicators, or time-based criteria. Additionally, practicing sound risk management principles, such as position sizing and risk-reward analysis, can help ensure that potential losses are kept in check.

Staying informed about market news, developments, and emerging trends is essential for proactive risk management. By staying abreast of the latest information, investors can anticipate market-moving events and adjust their strategies accordingly. Moreover, being aware of regulatory changes and geopolitical developments can help investors navigate potential risks stemming from external factors.

In conclusion, effective risk management is essential for navigating the volatile altcoin market successfully. By implementing strategies such as portfolio diversification, setting clear investment goals, conducting due diligence, and practicing disciplined trading, investors can mitigate potential losses and position themselves for long-term success. While the allure of altcoin investing may be strong, it's essential to approach it with caution and prudence, employing robust risk management strategies to safeguard capital in the face of uncertainty.

Chapter 3.2 - Portfolio Diversification

Portfolio Diversification: The ebook guides readers in developing a diversified altcoin portfolio, emphasizing its importance for long-term investment success and reducing overall risk exposure.

Crafting a Resilient Altcoin Portfolio: The Power of Diversification

In the fast-paced and exhilarating world of cryptocurrency investing, altcoins represent a realm of boundless opportunities. However, with these opportunities come inherent risks, as the altcoin market is renowned for its volatility and unpredictability. To navigate this landscape successfully and achieve long-term investment success, it is crucial for investors to embrace the principle of portfolio diversification.

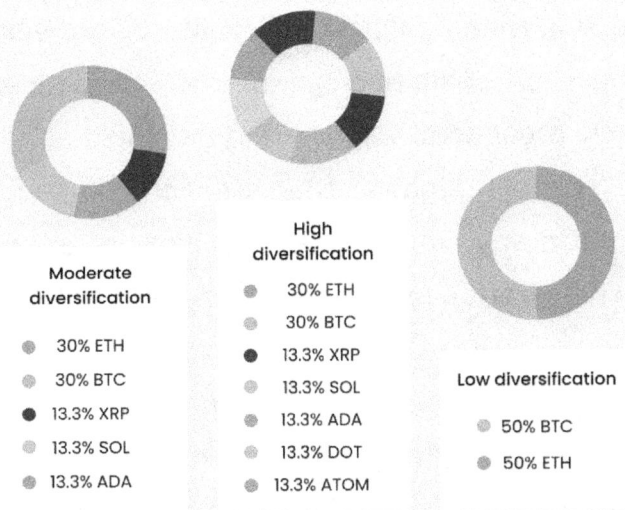

"Diversifying Your Altcoin Portfolio: A Guide to Long-Term Success" is an ebook designed to equip readers with the knowledge and tools necessary to develop a diversified altcoin portfolio. By emphasizing the importance of diversification and providing practical insights into its implementation, this guide empowers investors to reduce overall risk exposure and enhance the resilience of their investment strategies.

At its core, portfolio diversification involves spreading investments across a range of assets with different risk profiles and return potentials. In the context of altcoin investing, this means allocating capital to a diverse selection of altcoins, each exhibiting unique characteristics, use cases, and growth prospects. By diversifying their altcoin holdings, investors can mitigate the impact of adverse price movements in any single asset and capture opportunities for growth across various segments of the market.

The ebook begins by exploring the rationale behind portfolio diversification and its role in mitigating risk. Through illustrative examples and real-world case studies, readers gain a deeper understanding of how diversification can enhance investment resilience and smooth out portfolio volatility over time. Emphasizing the principle of "not putting all your eggs in one basket," the guide underscores the importance of spreading risk and avoiding over-concentration in any single asset or sector.

Next, the ebook provides practical guidance on how to construct a diversified altcoin portfolio. From defining investment objectives and risk tolerance levels to conducting thorough research and due diligence on potential investments, readers learn the essential steps involved in portfolio construction. By balancing factors such as asset allocation, sector exposure, and correlation analysis, investors can tailor their portfolios to reflect their individual goals and preferences while minimizing risk.

Furthermore, the ebook delves into advanced diversification strategies, such as rebalancing and tactical asset allocation. By periodically reassessing portfolio composition and adjusting allocations based on changing market conditions, investors can maintain optimal risk-return profiles and capitalize on emerging opportunities. Additionally, the guide explores the role of alternative assets, such as stablecoins and digital tokens, in diversifying risk and preserving capital during periods of market turbulence.

Throughout the ebook, emphasis is placed on the importance of a long-term perspective and disciplined investment approach. By focusing on the fundamentals of each altcoin investment and resisting the temptation of short-term speculation, investors can build robust portfolios capable of weathering market fluctuations and delivering sustainable returns over time.

In conclusion, "Diversifying Your Altcoin Portfolio" serves as a comprehensive guide to developing a resilient investment strategy in the altcoin market. By embracing the principles of portfolio diversification and applying practical insights into portfolio construction, readers can reduce overall risk exposure, enhance investment resilience, and position themselves for long-term success in the dynamic world of cryptocurrency investing.

Chapter 4 - Navigating Regulatory Challenges

Navigating Regulatory Challenges: It addresses regulatory challenges and legal considerations associated with altcoin investments, helping readers stay compliant and informed about relevant regulations.

Navigating Regulatory Challenges in Altcoin Investments: A Comprehensive Guide to Compliance and Legal Considerations

As the cryptocurrency market continues to evolve and mature, regulatory scrutiny has become an increasingly prominent issue for investors, particularly those venturing into the altcoin space. Altcoin investments, while offering exciting opportunities for growth and innovation, are subject to a complex web of regulatory frameworks and legal considerations that can vary significantly across jurisdictions. To navigate these challenges effectively and ensure compliance, investors must be well-informed about relevant regulations and proactive in their approach to legal compliance.

"Navigating Regulatory Challenges in Altcoin Investments" is a comprehensive guide designed to equip readers with the knowledge and tools necessary to navigate the regulatory landscape effectively. By addressing key regulatory challenges and legal considerations associated with altcoin investments, this guide empowers investors to stay compliant, mitigate regulatory risks, and make informed decisions in a rapidly changing regulatory environment.

The guide begins by providing an overview of the regulatory landscape governing altcoin investments, highlighting the diverse approaches taken by different jurisdictions around the world. From securities regulations to anti-money laundering (AML) and know-your-customer (KYC) requirements, readers gain insights into the regulatory frameworks that may impact their altcoin investments and the potential implications for compliance.

Next, the guide explores the classification of altcoins under various regulatory frameworks, distinguishing between security tokens, utility tokens, and payment tokens. Understanding the regulatory classification of altcoins is essential for determining the applicable regulatory requirements and compliance obligations, as different types of tokens may be subject to different regulatory regimes.

Furthermore, the guide delves into the legal considerations surrounding altcoin investments, including issues such as intellectual property rights, privacy concerns, data protection regulations, and contractual agreements. By addressing these legal considerations proactively, investors can mitigate legal risks and protect their interests when engaging in altcoin transactions and partnerships.

One of the key challenges facing altcoin investors is regulatory uncertainty, as the regulatory landscape continues to evolve rapidly in response to technological innovation and market developments. The guide provides strategies for navigating regulatory uncertainty, including staying informed about regulatory updates, engaging with regulators and industry stakeholders, and seeking legal counsel when needed.

Moreover, the guide emphasizes the importance of compliance with anti-money laundering (AML) and know-your-customer (KYC) regulations in the altcoin space. By implementing robust AML and KYC procedures, investors can mitigate the risk of regulatory enforcement actions and protect against potential reputational damage associated with illicit activities.

In addition to regulatory compliance, the guide addresses tax considerations related to altcoin investments, including the taxation of altcoin transactions, capital gains tax implications, and reporting requirements for cryptocurrency holdings. By understanding the tax implications of their altcoin investments, investors can ensure compliance with tax laws and optimize their tax planning strategies.

Throughout the guide, emphasis is placed on the importance of adopting a proactive approach to regulatory compliance and staying informed about relevant regulations and legal developments. By prioritizing compliance and adopting best practices for legal risk management, investors can navigate regulatory challenges effectively and safeguard their altcoin investments in a rapidly evolving regulatory landscape.

In conclusion, "Navigating Regulatory Challenges in Altcoin Investments" serves as a valuable resource for investors seeking to understand and address the regulatory and legal considerations associated with altcoin investments. By providing insights into key regulatory challenges, legal considerations, and compliance strategies, this guide empowers investors to navigate the regulatory landscape confidently, mitigate regulatory risks, and make informed decisions in the altcoin market.

Chapter 5 - Future Outlook and Emerging Technologies

Future Outlook and Emerging Technologies: The book explores the future of altcoins, discussing potential advancements and the impact of emerging technologies on the market, providing readers with foresight into upcoming developments.

Exploring the Future of Altcoins: Emerging Technologies and Potential Advancements

In the ever-evolving landscape of cryptocurrency, altcoins represent a realm of innovation and possibility, offering investors the opportunity to participate in groundbreaking technologies and disrupt traditional industries. As the altcoin market continues to evolve, it is essential for investors to stay ahead of the curve and anticipate future developments that may shape the trajectory of the market. "Future Outlook and Emerging Technologies in Altcoins" is a comprehensive book that delves into the future of altcoins, exploring potential advancements and the impact of emerging technologies on the market. By providing readers with foresight into upcoming developments, this book empowers investors to make informed decisions and capitalize on opportunities in the dynamic altcoin space.

The book begins by examining the current state of the altcoin market and identifying key trends and challenges facing the industry. From scalability issues to regulatory uncertainty, readers gain insights into the factors shaping the evolution of the altcoin market and the opportunities for growth and innovation that lie ahead.

Next, the book explores emerging technologies that have the potential to revolutionize the altcoin market and drive future advancements. From blockchain scalability solutions to interoperability protocols and decentralized finance (DeFi) platforms, readers learn about the latest developments shaping the future of altcoins and the potential impact on market dynamics.

One of the key areas of focus is the role of blockchain interoperability in enabling seamless communication and interaction between different blockchain networks. By facilitating interoperability, emerging technologies such as cross-chain bridges and interoperability protocols hold the potential to unlock new use cases and applications for altcoins, driving adoption and innovation in the market.

Moreover, the book explores the growing importance of decentralized finance (DeFi) and its potential to disrupt traditional financial services. From decentralized exchanges to lending and borrowing platforms, readers gain insights into the latest trends and developments in the DeFi space and the opportunities for altcoin investors to participate in this burgeoning ecosystem.

In addition to technological advancements, the book examines the potential impact of regulatory developments and macroeconomic trends on the future of altcoins. From regulatory clarity to geopolitical tensions and macroeconomic instability, readers gain insights into the external factors that may influence the trajectory of the altcoin market and the strategies for navigating potential risks and opportunities.

Throughout the book, emphasis is placed on the importance of staying informed and adaptable in the face of rapid technological innovation and market evolution. By understanding the latest developments and trends shaping the future of altcoins, investors can position themselves strategically and capitalize on opportunities for growth and innovation in the dynamic altcoin market.

In conclusion, "Future Outlook and Emerging Technologies in Altcoins" serves as a valuable resource for investors seeking to anticipate future developments and capitalize on opportunities in the altcoin space. By exploring emerging technologies, potential advancements, and the impact of regulatory and macroeconomic trends, this book empowers readers to stay ahead of the curve and make informed decisions in the evolving world of altcoin investing.

Chapter 6 – A Case Study

Title: The Rise and Fall of XYZ Coin: A Case Study in Altcoin Dynamics

Introduction:

XYZ Coin emerged in early 2018 amidst the fervor of the cryptocurrency boom. Promising revolutionary blockchain technology and ambitious use cases, it quickly captured the attention of investors worldwide. This case study delves into the journey of XYZ Coin, from its meteoric rise to its eventual decline, shedding light on the intricacies of the altcoin market.

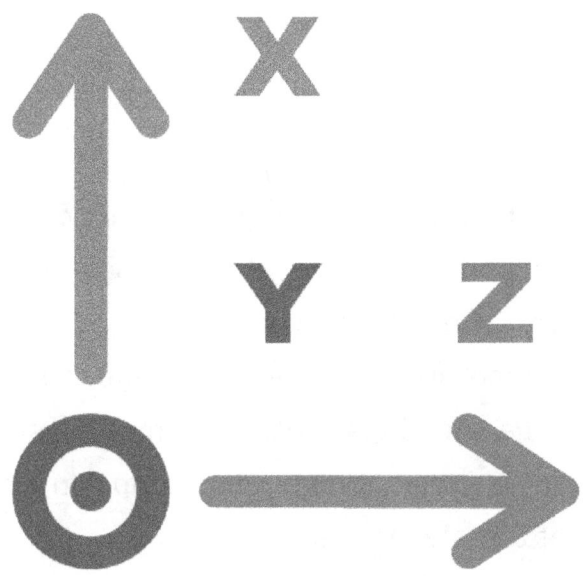

Background:

Founded by a team of seasoned developers, XYZ Coin entered the market with a bold vision: to disrupt the supply chain industry by leveraging blockchain technology. With a robust whitepaper outlining its decentralized platform for tracking goods from production to delivery, XYZ Coin garnered significant interest from both investors and industry players.

Rapid Ascent:

In the early months following its launch, XYZ Coin experienced exponential growth. Riding the wave of optimism surrounding cryptocurrencies, its value soared, attracting a diverse array of investors eager to capitalize on its potential. Partnerships with prominent supply chain companies further fueled excitement, propelling XYZ Coin to the forefront of the altcoin market.

Challenges and Controversies:

However, as XYZ Coin gained momentum, it also encountered its fair share of challenges. Concerns arose regarding the scalability and security of its blockchain, leading to doubts among investors and industry experts. Moreover, rumors of internal strife within the development team cast a shadow over the project's viability, sparking debates about its long-term prospects.

Market Volatility and Speculation:

Despite these obstacles, XYZ Coin continued to experience wild fluctuations in value, driven in part by speculation and market sentiment. Price pumps and dumps became commonplace, as traders sought to capitalize on short-term price movements. This volatility further eroded confidence in XYZ Coin's stability and reliability as an investment vehicle.

Regulatory Headwinds:

As XYZ Coin navigated the tumultuous waters of the altcoin market, it also faced increasing scrutiny from regulatory authorities. Concerns about potential violations of securities laws and lack of regulatory compliance loomed large, prompting investigations and enforcement actions. This regulatory uncertainty further dampened investor enthusiasm and contributed to XYZ Coin's downward trajectory.

Decline and Disillusionment:

Despite efforts to address its underlying issues, XYZ Coin ultimately succumbed to the harsh realities of the altcoin market. Its value plummeted, erasing gains for early investors and leaving a trail of disillusionment in its wake. The project, once hailed as a disruptive force in the supply chain industry, faltered under the weight of unfulfilled promises and dashed expectations.

Lessons Learned:

The case of XYZ Coin serves as a cautionary tale for participants in the altcoin market. It highlights the importance of thorough due diligence, transparent communication, and adherence to regulatory guidelines. Moreover, it underscores the need for realistic expectations and a long-term perspective when evaluating altcoin investments.

Conclusion:

As the dust settles on the rise and fall of XYZ Coin, it offers valuable insights into the dynamics of the altcoin market. While the allure of revolutionary technology and financial opportunity may be enticing, it is essential to approach altcoin investments with caution and skepticism. By learning from past successes and failures, investors can navigate the complexities of the altcoin landscape more effectively and make informed decisions that align with their risk tolerance and investment goals.

Chapter 7 - Conclusions

In conclusion, the world of altcoins represents both an exciting frontier and a terrain fraught with complexities and uncertainties. As we've journeyed through the pages of this ebook, we've explored the diverse landscape of alternative cryptocurrencies, delving into their origins, technologies, market dynamics, and potential future trajectories.

One undeniable truth emerges: altcoins have transformed the financial landscape, challenging traditional notions of currency, investment, and decentralized governance. From the pioneering days of Bitcoin to the proliferation of thousands of altcoins, each with its unique value proposition, we've witnessed a remarkable evolution in the way we conceive of and interact with money and assets.

However, this evolution has not been without its challenges. The altcoin market is rife with volatility, speculation, and, at times, outright scams. The allure of quick riches has drawn in both seasoned investors and newcomers alike, often leading to euphoria and disappointment in equal measure.

Moreover, the regulatory environment surrounding altcoins remains uncertain and subject to rapid change. Governments and policymakers grapple with how to classify, regulate, and tax these digital assets, further complicating the landscape for investors and enthusiasts.

Yet, amid these challenges, there is cause for optimism. Altcoins continue to push the boundaries of innovation, driving forward groundbreaking technologies such as smart contracts, decentralized finance (DeFi), non-fungible tokens (NFTs), and more. These advancements hold the potential to revolutionize not just finance but also industries ranging from gaming to healthcare to supply chain management.

Furthermore, altcoins offer an unprecedented level of financial inclusion, empowering individuals around the world with access to banking and investment opportunities previously out of reach. Cryptocurrencies have the potential to level the playing field, providing a means for the unbanked and underbanked to participate in the global economy.

As we look to the future of altcoins, it is clear that their journey is far from over. While the road ahead may be uncertain, one thing remains certain: innovation will continue to drive progress in this dynamic and rapidly evolving space. Whether it's the emergence of new consensus mechanisms, the integration of privacy features, or the exploration of novel use cases, altcoins will continue to shape the future of finance and technology.

In this ever-changing landscape, one principle remains paramount: due diligence. As investors and enthusiasts, it is imperative that we approach the world of altcoins with a critical eye, conducting thorough research, and exercising caution in our endeavors. By staying informed, remaining vigilant, and embracing the spirit of innovation responsibly, we can navigate the complexities of the altcoin market and unlock its vast potential for the benefit of all.

www.ingramcontent.com/pod-product-compliance
Lightning Source LLC
Chambersburg PA
CBHW050246230526

45470CB00005B/2143